Four Letter Words

Brittney Harrell

BookLeaf
Publishing

India | USA | UK

Presentation by *BookLeaf Publishing*

Web: www.bookleafpub.com

E-mail: info@bookleafpub.com

ISBN: 9789363300408

First edition 2024

To Amir, and all with four letter names.

June

The thunderstorm signified the fun was starting
soon
Cigarettes and Smirnoff as we gazed up at the
moon
We walked home late at night knowing you'll
call me out at noon
I was such a fool back then
And every day I'd see you,
You'd remind me that your leaving
Across the world for the next month,
Would you like me to be grieving?
Something that looks a lot like love
Won't look that way this evening
Won't look that way in June
In the afternoon
you adored me

Fire

2

There's a wildfire 100 miles away.
The air is thick, the sky ash gray
The hours flew past and blended the day
Advisory alerts on the news but nothing else to
say

Stay

I didn't want to remember you
Because the way you shut me out was so cold
I didn't want to admit defeat but I had to hold
my feelings
Though you sent a text on every holiday
and random occasion
What did it matter?
If you weren't ready to leave

Wine

4

Deeper in color than any darkness from the night
The night you made me so disappointed in
myself

Glad

5

It's only in the summer do I pine
For you
A to-do list a million miles long but I'd still
make time for you
I'm sure you realize, as an adult, that childish
isn't the word to describe what you were doing
before.
Pouring liquor down my throat until I was
unconscious on the floor.
so glad we are past that
So glad I stayed fat
to avoid the affection you only give the thin
Me documenting every single moment with a
ball point pen, because these memories can't be
erased.
Or undone
Your guilt burning as hot as the sun

Ruby

6

What was it you said?
It's white
It's red
It's begging you to wake up so you'll come to
bed
The nightmares behind you still filling you with
dread
Subliminal reminders that the old you is dead

Even

You should be grateful I know of something
higher than myself
To take care of us while you chase wealth
Ignoring everything, including your health
What on earth are you thinking about?
A less patient person would clap right back at
the early morning snaps
And let you know where to store your apology
Say sorry like you mean it
There is no automatic sympathy anymore, you'll
have to redeem it

Gasp

My thoughts are not my own
In this moment
Almost violent, we'll condone it
And set the new standard
My thoughts are not my own
In this second
Caution to the wind, in the car, we'll wreck it
before we give something else the attention.

Not my own, because it all belongs to you in this
moment.

Brat

Nothing like a spoiled brat
Spoiled meaning you've never heard a no
Brat meaning you'll resort to violence to change
the answer
And brat out when you can't change the
outcome
How many years did you spend talking shit
about my country?
Join the club of millions
Everyone much to old to baby you or deal with
your attitude
So you never learned to scale it back
And it yanked you from your family, just like
that
Foreigners love foreigners who are nothing but
trouble
Not sorry you had to realize it the hard way
A promise you broke because the coke couldn't
keep it for you
Crying for the time you'll never get back
The people you'll never get back
The condition of your liver you'll have to get on
track
But first, you'll need to stop.

Slay

Quiet slay
contemplation on your face
The filter in your mouth
Our auras do a little race
Acknowledge that the moment is gone

Play

Every animal next to us
Is a sign of something better
Proof of new life or
The right track
Every night you spend on the couch
Is a question of existential proportions
Multi dimensional questions that transform
space and time because it really is that deep
Reliving every bad moment as you toss and turn
in your sleep
Yearning for the crisp air that spells out October
Time is ticking
Play time is over

Lime

If you didn't see life as fragile before
You should now
All the signs around you
We even know how
But we gamble with consequences
That are very real to everyone
And ignore it by proving that point with
substance

Liar

In what universe does that make sense?
Be a little more descriptive
Doesn't sound like you
How many friends were you with and what did
dinner come to?
For you to sit there and make me think that your
words were true
Glaring through my sunglasses as the elevator,
the stairs, our lives take us higher
The L word is forbidden but your pants are on
fire.

July

There was no sizzle
But the heat was felt
Searing the bare feet
Waiting for the flesh to melt
All the nylon is bleached
The ice beseeched
Record-breaking temperatures
Skin burning all week

Here

Beryl is hitting Houston
The asteroid just flew by
It's 120 in Palm Springs this week
Looking for the colors in the sky

It flooded in Dubai this spring
His brother had water up to his knees
This would be the time for the Tacoma
But we don't have the keys.

I'm sure it's raining love in Bermuda
And any other place that isn't here.

More

Can you be a good friend if you ask for more?
More support
More encouragement
More than you bargained for
Cheerleading for other ideas
Instead of expanding your own

Paid

9% profit reporting
But my whole team leaves in August
Here I am wishing I should have stayed
You should be more modest
Your excitement seems contained at the thought
of opportunity
It's just so soon to me
Muscle memory at my operator id
Every script I see
Every problem on the feed
Money came Wednesday, let's times it by three
Big deposits of money are attracted to me

Slum

The showers are leaking
The toilets run
The ceiling is drooping
The faucets are done

The stove is old
The fridge is loud
The blinds are filthy
But you're proud

If we exploited you, there would be no chaser,
no puzzles, no hints
You are sneakily exploiting me by not lowering
the rent, knowing that your house is falling
apart.

Good

You exceeded every expectation I thought you could
Prancing around like you couldn't be caught
I know you want to call but I don't think you should
Regret is worth more than anything you've ever bought
Asking you to share your feelings but you never would
Summer is ending and I haven't heard from you
That's good
I'm good.

Rain

Hotter now than it was
Today, when a pink rainbow wrapped the city
Like a sign from God
Or a thank you or a acknowledgement that you
see us and love us
The air is hot
But the wind is cooler
And the rum is taking us away
It rained last night but if you blinked, you may
have missed it.

Holy

Dear Heavenly Father,
I thank you for the trees
The sunshine and fresh air
I'm grateful for the breeze
The trees leaning sideways,
Weighted down with fruit
Amongst the new baby foliage
Not yet taken root
What a gift we have inherited
Amongst all the dirt
We move on but still cry because we can't hide
our hurt
I move along on the path of righteousness
because I see my future in paradise
Confirmed through the means of which I know
you, through your son, through his love of the
world, which wraps around us, forever.

9 789363 300408